In Celebration of Women
poems by *Coomi Singh*

To Jessica,
With all good wishes.
Coomi Singh
9-12-2003

Vakils, Feffer & Simons Pvt. Ltd.,
Hague Building, 9 Sprott Road, Ballard Estate,
Mumbai 400 001, India.

Supported by Aditya Vikram Birla Memorial Trust.

Pictures courtesy Ms. Niloufer Wadia. Visit www.niloufer.com for more of Niloufer's art.

Monies received for this book will be used by:

(1)   The Dinshaw J. Amaria Memorial Foundation towards health and nutrition facilities for needy children.

(2)   PASSAGES Association for Guidance, Education & Support for their cancer related activities.

Donations to The Dinshaw J. Amaria Memorial Foundation and PASSAGES are exempt U/S 80G of the Income Tax Act (1961), India.

Institutions or individuals wishing to help these Charities by placing bulk orders for gifting this book may write to:

Dr. Coomi Singh, Trustee
The Dinshaw J. Amaria Memorial Foundation
1A, Greenfield, Ground Floor, 40, S. V. Road
Santacruz (West), Mumbai 400 054.

Price: Rs. 260/-; US $ 11.95.

Published by
Bimal A. Mehta at Vakils, Feffer & Simons Pvt. Ltd.,
Hague Building, 9 Sprott Road, Ballard Estate, Mumbai 400 001, India.

Printed by
Arun K. Mehta at Vakil & Sons Pvt. Ltd., Industry Manor,
Appasaheb Marathe Marg, Worli, Mumbai-400 025. India.

ISBN No.: 81-87111-65-8.

ABOUT THE AUTHOR

Born in Hubli, Karnataka, Coomi has lived all her life in Mumbai, a city she is passionate about. She has an M.Phil (Sociology) and Ph.D. (Sociology) degree and over the years has organized and conducted several programmes for different organizations, including the International Labour Organization and Bombay Management Association where she was the Chairperson of the Women in Management Committee (1998-99), among others.

Currently, she is studying 'The Social and Emotional Impact of Cancer on the Patient and in the Family' for PASSAGES, an NGO which has become an integral part of her life.

Coomi is also Founder Trustee of The Dinshaw J. Amaria Memorial Foundation, established in the memory of her father, and Trustee of the Lady Engineer High School, Tardeo.

Her interests include reading, writing poetry, and stories for children and articles on topics of interest to her, travel, movies and meeting people.

Her message to the younger generation is: Be dynamic and devote at least 10% of your time to activities of human interest, community and the nation. Make time for it. Where there is a will, there is a way!

FOREWORD

I still remember a young girl of four, dark curly hair and eyes "like saucers" who wrote her first poem and went to show it to her parents. The poem was:

I have a puppy
> Whose name is Duppy
> Duppy is good
> He eats a lot of food
> He even eats bones
> His surname is Jones.

Those parents never laughed at her. They took her poem seriously and told her it was wonderful. They encouraged her to write. Those were my parents. They made me feel that I was a genius or child prodigy. I felt really good about myself. That was the beginning of my love affair with poetry.

Whenever a subject moves me deeply, I want to rush to put my feelings down on paper in poetry, the most recent event being the tragic demise of Kalpana Chawla and her colleagues in the destruction of the Columbia.

Some five years ago, a good friend introduced me to Tarana, Kaya and Valerie who were just launching an NGO called 'PASSAGES'. The concept, and their commitment and dedication touched the very core of my heart and I have always felt, like them, that PASSAGES is 'my baby' too. I had not really written any poetry for some time being caught up in routine matters, when Kaya asked me to write a poem on PASSAGES. Sitting at the computer, I thought, "What should I write?" As if by divine intervention, words flowed, and I wrote the poem 'Woman' for PASSAGES. Again, the appreciation I received from everybody when it was published in the PASSAGES Newsletter spurred me on and I ended up writing more than fifty poems in celebration of Women.

My Ph.D. degree is in 'Women's Studies', done under the guidance of Dr. Neera Desai, a well-respected teacher and author of several books on women's issues. Apart from this, I have done some research on issues concerning women, including one for the International Labour Organisation, which took me to several countries in South Asia. These poems are a culmination of my interest in womanhood and my love for poetry.

This book would not have been possible in its current format without the support of several people. My sincere and grateful thanks to Mrs. Rajashree Birla for her gracious generosity and encouragement, Ms. Niloufer Wadia for readily permitting me to use her pictures for the noble cause of charities, Mr. Arun Mehta and his team at Vakils, Ms. Suyogita Dandekar, Mr. Ram Giri for his hours of devoted and patient labour, my friends at PASSAGES – a constant source of inspiration, and last but not least, to my family for believing in me.

Coomi Singh

PREFACE

It is a matter of dual pleasure for me to welcome Dr. Coomi Singh's collection of poems, 'In Celebration of Women' in the arena of expression of women's voices. A teacher experiences great joy when her student is traversing newer fields. Further, Dr. Singh, through her first publication of poems, expresses her perception and sensitivity to issues enveloping women's lives.

In the widening horizon of women's studies in different directions and varied disciplines, literature has been a significant area of concern. The present collection, while depicting various facets of women's lives, also, to my mind, reveals the gradual development of sensitivity of the poet. Starting with the visible, outward features of women's body, slowly Dr. Singh enters the nuances of relationships of woman as a daughter, sister, wife, mother and grandmother. Moving from individual to social is a major stride for a gender conscious artist.

The qualities of inner strength, resilience, courage or power are not merely celebrated in an individual coping with myriads of challenges of the inner and outer world, but have been gradually articulated in sympathetic understanding of social dimensions of women's issues in poems like 'On Rape', 'The Girl Child', 'Child Bride' and 'Prostitution'.

I hope that Dr. Singh will continue this pursuit with vigour, mature expression and sensitive commitment.

Dr. Neera Desai
Sociologist
Professor & Former Head of the
Department of Sociology
S.N.D.T. University, Mumbai

CONTENTS

An Indian Bride

I see you and I am reminded of spring
Of vibrant colour and beautiful things.
Radiant, glowing, resplendent in red
Mysterious and magical, vermilion on your head.

I see you and I am struck with awe
Beautiful maiden, innocent and pure.
Eyes lowered in shyness, a delight to behold
From head to toe, bedecked in gold.

I see you and thank God from deep down inside
What have I done to deserve you by my side?
Beautiful maiden, may I never forget
God gave you to me and so I'm doubly blest.

An Indian Beauty

I passed her in the market place
The whiff of her perfume as she glided by
Such beauty I have never seen
Raven hair and dark brown eyes.

Translucent skin and straight long limbs
Her gait so fair as she drifted by
The slender waist and delicate ankles
Her sari gently caressing her thighs.

The sweet jingle of bells on her slender feet
Tall and graceful and modestly shy
Oh Indian woman, I have yet to see
Such beauty as thine!

Mehndi

Hands folded in front of her
Greeting the traditional way
Covered with intricate henna.
What the hands say is 'Namaste'.

Long fingers, beautifully manicured
Soft and supple and gentle
Full of grace and beauty pure
Captivating, mystical, magical.

The mehndi bright red and bold
"Her husband will love her a lot",
And so o'er the years, it's been told,
"If the henna clings and fades not."

The young bride, watching anxiously
Will the colour take or not?
Will he treat her lovingly?
The mehndi reveals, what?

Old wive's tales, and tricks and such
To make the young bride feel
Like a fairytale princess with good luck
Waiting for her prince, their love to seal.

ॐ☙

- "Mehndi" is 'henna' that is applied on the Indian woman's hand during ceremonies.
- "Namaste" is the traditional Indian way of greeting, with folded hands.

Love At First Sight

Every morning
On my way to work
I pass by your house
Looking up
At your balcony
There you are standing
Raven hair
Cascading to your knee
Eyes large with the joy of living.

Beautiful maiden
My heart is throbbing
Do you feel what I feel?
Every day
You watch me passing
Do your heartbeats feel a thrill?
Blood pounding
In my veins, I stare
I stare openly and unashamedly.

Such beauty
O lovely Indian woman
You are indeed a treat, a feast
For eyes
That thirst for a look
From you. Look at me, what do you see?
A man
Lovesick, longing to protect
To put you on a pedestal, yet keep you free.

$\infty \infty$

Beauty

A hint of a smile on her lips
As she passes me by

The rhythmic sway of her hips
Face, coy and shy

Warmth and laughter in her eyes
Deep pools of love

Sari folds, caressing her slender thighs
An angel, from above

Her bosom, full and firm
A heart within

Woman, to you I turn
You are the sun

৵৹

Seductress

Voluptuous, airing your charms
Curvaceous, inviting and warm
Lips parted slightly
The hint of a smile
As pearly teeth gleam in the sun.

Sari clad so tightly around
Clinging to hips, well shaped and round
The tinkle of bells
As you cast your spell
Each time you move, your payals sound.

Your look is oh so tender
Your arms long and slender
Hold me in your arms
Hold me in your arms
I cannot resist. I surrender!

❧❧

Adoration

So many songs have been sung
In praise of women
Songs of adoration, songs of love
Songs of beauty and devotion.

Woman as goddess
Woman as mother
Woman as wife
Sister to her brother.

Woman, the mighty
Woman, the true
Steadfast and loyal
An anchor for you.

Woman, the seductress
Woman, the tramp
Woman, the gentle
The lady with the lamp.

The bearer of life
The pillar at home
Woman is 'Shakti'
Resilient and strong.

So I too sing these songs for you
Oh woman, in praise
The world would end without you
Extinct, the human race!

'Shakti': The Indian word for 'Strength'.

My Beloved Wife

That day in our lives so long ago
I live that memory over and over again in my head
You gave me your heart and all your love
You came to my home and shared my bed.

From the moment we pledged our love
In front of the priests and our folks and our friends
I have never felt afraid or alone
You are my wife, my lover, my solace, my confidante.

We've shared so much together
The two of us; sorrow and grief, happiness and joy
Sickness and health, work and recreation
And the thrill of our children, our girl and our boy.

Now more than twenty five years later
Approaching the twilight of our lives, I still feel
A surge of emotion; you are my anchor
My beloved wife, without you I wouldn't be.

❧

To A Great Lady, My Teacher

My teacher, my guru
I never told you so
Inspiration came from you
And spurred me on for more.

Your academic brilliance
The depth of your emotion
The wealth of your experience
Have spurred me on to action.

It's strange how very often
When thoughts are in confusion
A chat with you will soften
And wipe out all commotion.

My teacher, my guru
I hear you with devotion
I respect and revere you
So does this grateful nation.

જ∽ઙ

This poem is dedicated to my teacher Dr. Neera Desai who was Head of the Sociology Dept. at SNDT Women's University, Mumbai.

Mother

Mother, you bore me in your womb for nine long months,
You lumbered along, never complaining of pain.
Swollen ankles, nausea, backache and such
Yet you told me that you would have done it again.

You told me that when you held me in your arms
You shook with emotion, your joy was complete.
This wrinkled and tiny, "bundle of joy"
An expression of the love that you and father feel.

As I grew up I watched you, Mother, always there
So loving, so understanding, so patient and kind.
You went on and on selflessly toiling for us
A mother, a friend, you could read into my mind.

The touch of your hand on a fevered brow
The brush of your lips, the love in your eyes.
The "pillar of our home" as father always says
Mother, O Mother, the strength of your smile.

I have learned from you so much, O Mother mine
That I am confident I will grow up to become
A good citizen, a decent and loving human being
Contributing to society and all of mankind.

A Mother's Love

A Jewish folktale tells us
That a mother's love will last
The beloved has asked her betrothed
To bring his mother's heart.

The son tears out that loving heart
And he races to his beloved
But on the way he stumbles and falls
And the heart is doubly wounded.

As he lifts himself, his mother's voice
From the bleeding heart enquires
"Did you hurt yourself, my beloved son?
Is there anything you require?"

Grandmother

That beautiful lady with the silvery hair
Is my grandmother. Do you see her squatting there?
Do you see how she is stooped with age?
How her knobby fingers still work in frenzied rage?

Making papads, chapattis, pickles and such
Day long she works. How does she do so much?
I remember when I was just a little girl
Looking for solace, she'd pass her fingers through my curls.

On that fateful day of the accident
My mother died. Under the wheels of a car her life went.
Her only daughter so cruelly taken from her
But she hid her hurt and wiped my tears away.

It was a long time ago, I was only nine
It was she, my grandmother, who gave me all her time.
She fed me, she taught me, she loved me a lot
In sickness and health, whether good times or not.

I am soon to be married and will go away
What will become of Grandma? Who will with her stay?
I keep telling her that I do not want to marry
She laughs at me and says, "Sweet child, do not worry."

In her wisdom she says she will soon be gone
Her life has been hard and her life has been long
It would fill her loving heart for sure
To know I was safe and well provided for.

My grateful heart is overflowing with devotion
For her. Love so eternal, memories set in motion.
She gives me her love unconditional and true
Grandmother, all I want is to be like you.

Woman As Mother

Have you seen the face of a woman
As she holds her infant in her arms?
Such love, such rapture, such enchantment
Writ on her face as she gazes, charmed.

Have you noticed the pain of a woman
As her young one lies ill in her arms?
Such anxiety, such patience, such devotion
Nursing, tending, keeping her loved one warm.

Have you felt the thrill of a woman
When her child comes home with achievement?
Such pride, such joy, such elation
Such news for sharing is meant.

Have you sensed the emotion of a woman
As she gazes on her young daughter, the bride?
Feelings so mixed, anxious, loving
Praying for the happiness of her child.

Have you known the love of a woman
Who holds her grandchild on her knee?
Her peace, her knowledge, her wisdom
Her blessings and love plain to see.

Have you seen the many faces of woman
In her capacity and role of mother?
A mother's love is universal
Not related to wealth or culture.

Sisters

The four sisters who love each other
Remember the days gone by
When they were young and in their parents' home
And their childhood filled with joy.

Steadfast loyalty and devotion
The sisters' love is true
They stand by each other through thick and thin
The power of such love, what it can do!

Far away from each other
Distanced by many miles
But ever near each other in mind and heart
As they lead their married lives.

A sister is also a friend
And so are these to each other
Wherever they go they will always know
That their lives are bound together.

Bound by that golden thread
Of sisterly love and trust
Bonds of sisterhood, friendship, womanhood
Bonds that will always last.

ॐॐ

A Teenage Daughter

My little girl, you have grown up
You have blossomed and bloomed
Into a rose. What pride I have in you
When I see your grace and poise.

You are well mannered and gentle
You are good natured and true
Your youthful body firm and supple
I could go on gazing at you.

I look at your face and remember
The days of yesteryear
It seems that I am looking
Into an old mirror.

A daughter is also a friend
I thank God I have you
Now you are grown we can share
As two women, one to another.

જ્ઞજ્ઞ

A Good Wife

My beloved husband, I've tried to be
A good wife to you at all times
It is not just because I am a woman
And this is what is expected of me.

I love you with a love that is unending
Because you are a good man
You are kind and noble and true
You are a husband, loving and understanding.

So many years since we were young
You have touched me, I have grown
You have always encouraged me
No matter what the song I've sung.

You listen whenever I talk to you
Your broad shoulder is always available
I feel safe, protected and warm
When life gets me down or I'm feeling blue.

Our lives are bound together
Through eternity. If like the cat with nine lives
I would still choose only you
Forever and ever and ever.

A Good Mother

My daughter, what I have taught you
Is what I know to be right
I've made no difference ever
Because of your female gender.

My son, I have always told you
To be kind and loving and true
To be gentle with ladies and women
Not show off your physical acumen.

Violence is meant for self defence
When your safety has been threatened.
A daughter should not be cowed down
Face up to it and hold your own.

I have tried hard to be a good mother
And instill the right values in you
Remember always to respect each other
And to your own selves be true.

❦

30th Anniversary

I am a woman who
Thirty years ago
Pledged herself to you
Then and forever more.

How good life has been
God has blessed our love
So much of life we've seen
'Tis a blessing from above.

Ups and downs in life
Through thick and thin
Through stress and strife
Through it all we've been.

Two loving children
Through sickness and health
Through good times and bad
Our love is our wealth.

Ever strong it grows
Year after loving year
Dearest, I'm sure you know
I am yours forever.

≈∽

Nurture

A woman's natural tendency
Is to nurture
From the cradle to the grave
That is her nature.

Healing with a gentle touch
A woman's love
God could not be everywhere
He works thro' woman, from above.

Companionship

In the twilight of our lives
I am here for you
Day and night
I have always been
And will continue to be
Your constant companion.

In these, our sunset years
Memories cling
Of days gone by
While you and I sit
Holding hands and cherishing
Each precious moment that passes by.

A Woman's Love

The love of a woman
Have you ever known it?
From the time you were born
You have lived with it.

The hand that rocked your cradle
The lips that kissed your brow
The gentle heart that loved you well
And eased away your frown.

The grandma you always turned to
When things did not go your way
The woman who made you candy bars
And wiped your tears away.

The sister you grew up with
Who worships and admires you
She takes your taunts so lovingly
Even today her love is true.

The wife whose love is steadfast
Who has become a part of you
Your constant friend and companion
Your lover, your wife so true.

The love of a good woman
It is powerful and strong
It is love that can move mountains
It is love that makes life a song.

Pregnancy

Pregnant with hope
Joy, anticipation
Ecstasy, love
And deep devotion.

Will it be a boy or girl?
Will it be healthy?
Looking in the mirror
At her swollen belly.

Feeling the movements
Knowing quite well
A young life is budding
Relishing the thrill.

The aches and the pain
The swellings and such
Do not matter at all
She yearns for a touch.

A woman she is
Taking great strides
Doing God's work on earth
The bearer of life!

❧

My Granddaughter

New Year's eve, the turn of the century
Late in the night, my grandchild was born.
Beautiful, perfect, angelic, a dream!

Twenty minutes later, she was in my arms
And as I looked into her beautiful face
My heart swelled, I prayed.

Once more, in the true meaning of life, I find
God's miracle! Could anything be more joyous?
This precious gift, to make our lives sublime.

The Greatest Love

When we were bound together, man and wife
I promised I'd be your partner the rest of my life,
And so it has been these thirty years
Through sunshine and laughter
Through sorrow and tears.

And now, in our twilight years, together forever
Love has stayed steadfast, constant, beautiful and ever more tender.
Today, as we stand hand in hand, braving it all
We fight to conquer on the battlefield of cancer,
We fight for time, our love stands tall.

Look back at our life, how eventful it's been,
How much we have achieved, how much we have dreamed.
But life isn't over, there's still so much to do
Because you love me
And because I love you.

&oc&

Dedicated to my husband, Bharat, fighting for his life in the ICU at Breach Candy.

Grief

I understand your pain
I feel for you
Pain must come
But it will go
And life will be altered
But will continue to flow.

In these difficult times
I offer my love
My prayers are for you
To the Almighty above
May God give you both strength
And all the time that you want.

This poem is dedicated to a friend who, with courage and dignity, watched over her
terminally ill husband.

Comfort

Come into my open arms
Lay your head upon my breast
Hold me close
And you will soon find rest.

For I am a woman
I have so much love to give
Take all I have
I give so you can live.

Anyone will tell you
A woman's love is boundless
Without your words
I can feel your distress.

I promise you comfort
Rest your head in my lap
You will find peace
I promise you that.

৵৹

Nerves Of Steel

A woman, when faced with disaster
Illness, hardship, pain and terror
For those whom she loves, could easily be
Brave and bold, with nerves of steel.

When her husband is stressed or ailing
Her love and support, never failing
She is there for him and will always be
His very own woman, with nerves of steel.

Her son's had an accident, her daughter ill
A woman, God bless her, with unbending will
Sleepless, tireless, a driving force will be
This loving mother, with nerves of steel.

A cause she believes in, no matter what
That may help lighten the poor man's lot
A woman with conviction, she will ever be
A force to reckon with, with nerves of steel.

Males are strong, they say, physically so
A woman is delicate, gentle and pure
And yet, when put to the test, she will be
Emotionally resilient, with nerves of steel.

ॐॐ

Resilience

Gentle as the breeze
Slim and smaller built
Woman is all these
And yet resilient.

Quietly, silently strong
In her heart brave
All her life long
Courage is what it takes.

Untimely widowed
Children still small
Courage in hand
She braves it all.

Earning a salary
Caring for the kids
Facing the worries
Smiling, through all this.

O woman, how brave
You are, how silent
Thro' all your suffering
How resilient!

৵৽

This poem is dedicated to my mother, Dhun Dinshaw Amaria. My father passed away when she was only 49 years of age.

Woman

O woman, I sing this song in eternal praise of you
Your many faces, each one surpassing the other
Daughter, sister, wife, mother, friend, confidante...
All converge, O woman, into you.

You are the bearer of life, the keeper of souls
Your burden in life much greater than most
As you go through the various PASSAGES in your life
O woman, what do you dream of? What is your goal?

You are strong, resilient, faithful and true
And yet you were born to suffer indignity and shame
Female infanticide, dowry deaths, battering and more
O woman, these social PASSAGES you must go through!

Giving birth, coping with monthly PMS, HRT and stress
All that is related to your physical and mental health
You take it all in your stride with courage and strength
O woman, through all these PASSAGES you are no less.

You have come a long, long way, taking great strides
Engineer, doctor, lawyer, space woman, teacher, nurse
No field closed to you as you awaken to your promise and potential
O woman, you are this grateful nation's pride.

So woman, be bold and take your rightful place in this world
Let nothing or no one keep you down or hold you back
Hand in hand with your men folk, not lagging behind
Join forces, integrate, go forward, create a new world.

So woman, I salute you, I celebrate your grace
You go through the PASSAGES in your life with dignity
Your inner strength, your charm, your tender heart
O woman, O woman, I offer you praise!

(A poem written for PASSAGES, an NGO)

Substance

When I started on this project
Many people asked me
If I would have enough to write
On 'Woman' so much poetry.

But being a woman I knew
I was inspired to write
About you and me, about us
About our love and our might.

Is there any other subject
In this great, big world
That has created so much magic
But the woman or the girl?

Is there any life at all
In all of nature free
That hasn't been touched by
The female species?

Oh woman, you are strength
Anywhere and everywhere
Where there is love and tenderness
Oh woman, you are there.

A Common Purpose

A good friend invited me
And I went for a seminar on 'Emotional Depression'
A new NGO called "PASSAGES' was being launched.

"You will like these ladies"
She wrote to me. "Their work is close to your heart".
And so I went, a trifle reluctantly, and found my part.

Initially, hesitant and unsure
"Would I get on with these young women?" I thought
Instantly I knew and found myself caught.

Five years have passed
So much good work has been done and achieved
Social and legal issues, and helping to fight disease.

Empowering women
To fulfill their dreams and to become really aware
Of inner selves, and also what's available out there.

Parenting issues
Seminars, workshops and an informative newsletter
A telephone help line and support group for Cancer.

Great big strides
PASSAGES you have moved from small beginnings
Keep up the good work and your spirit ever soaring.

Achieve greater heights
Grow from strength to strength and find great glory
In your strength, so many women weave their story.

I salute you
Because you are beautiful and true at the very core
Your dedication and commitment, your purpose pure.

Patience

Patience is a virtue
Not very often found in this mad life
Who has time for another
In this life so full of strife?

Constantly striving
To outdo one another in this rat race
Where do you see patience?
You see it in a woman's face.

The face of the beloved
Awaiting her lover who sneaks in late
The face and stance of a wife
Who for her husband patiently waits.

The face of an anxious daughter
As she nurses her ailing parents
The face of the loving mother
Whose broken heart won't mend.

Patience is a woman
Anxiously awaiting her fate
Cajoled and beaten to silence
Enlightened and awakened so late!

Patiently waiting
For man to learn to accept
That with her beside him
So many tears need not have been wept.

৵৵

Courage

I see courage in her face
A dear friend
Radiant, beautiful, young
She looks so full of strength.

No one will ever know
Looking at her
The tragic story of pain
Beneath that bright exterior.

What is it that gives her
That extra strength?
It is her inner beauty
It is her resilience.

A wife, a mother loving
A friend too
Concerned for other's welfare
Will you not love her too?

Niloufer 2003

She sets a good example
To one and all
No matter what the odds are
She loves, and is loved well.

O, beautiful woman
May you ever be
Blessed with fortitude
And with your loved ones, happy.

This poem was inspired by a dear friend coping with cancer.

Woman Power

It is absolutely amazing
What can be achieved
When two or more women
Like-minded, begin
To think and act together.

Their combined strengths
Of womanly qualities
Of candour, loyalty, commitment
Steadfastness and dedication
Help to make life better.

And so, it sometimes happens
That a few such women
Combine energies to strengthen
And educate those less fortunate
To face all kinds of weather.

Women's groups are many
Each one working hard
To share experiences and lend
Support, a helping hand
Working by spirit and letter.

Then think, how much more forceful
How wonderfully strong and successful
If these women's groups combined
Their efforts through all times
And set an example through WOMAN POWER!

Great Heights of Glory

Brave daughter of India,
Kalpana Chawla,
How much you have achieved.
In a life so short,
With danger, fraught,
To the greatest heights you've reached.

You've made your mark in history,
Kalpana Chawla
Your name will ever be
One that inspires,
Fans the desire
To dare to fly, and to achieve.

A giant leap for womankind,
Kalpana Chawla,
You have shown the way!
Smiling and petite,
With nerves of steel,
Women like you are not born everyday.

The world grieves for you,
Kalpana Chawla
Our hearts are broken.
Those with you,
Who have perished too,
Tears for them in every nation.

In the arms of your Creator,
Kalpana Chawla,
Know that you have lived
A life, though brief,
Useful and complete,
A life worth emulating.

On Friendship

Men are from Mars, women from Venus
This book explains the reason
Women make such good friends
It speaks of their emotion.

A woman needs to talk
About all her problems
She wants you to listen to her
Not necessarily offer solutions.

She wants to feel loved and nurtured
A shoulder to rest her head on
Be patient, be kind and be gentle
Don't rush to find answers head on.

So, one woman to another
Such good friends they can become
They understand each other
They think and feel as one.

❧

Gender Differences

We hear so much every day
About gender differences
'She's a woman', they say
'No wonder she behaves this way'
'Why can't she be like me?'

Differences are necessary
To keep the balance in life
How dull our lives would be
Without differences, without you or me!
If everything was black and white!

Biological differences figure
In gender, most certainly
You are physically bigger
Broad shouldered and muscular
I feel safe and secure with thee.

But I am strong too
In a different way
I am gentle and true
I will always love you
With a love that will never sway.

When tackling a problem
You seek a solution immediately
You withdraw in your shell
Till something strikes a bell
And then you share it with me.

When I have a problem
I come running to you
To cry on your shoulder
To rest in your arms
To hear you say, 'I love you.'

Our gender differences
They balance our lives
Our strengths and our weaknesses
Designed by Divine purpose
To make our lives worthwhile.

Brides Are Not For Burning

With what hope I entered your home
I would be a good wife
I would do all that was expected of me
Never would you feel alone.

Barely a month had passed us by
You turned into someone else
You grumbled and found fault
You began to tell me lies.

Demanding a price for your love
"Bring money and gold or else....."
You hurled abuse at my parents
You began to hit and to shove.

Your mother would taunt me
Your father sit quiet
I couldn't' take these insults
I longed to be free.

Then, horror of horrors, you came
And doused me with kerosene
While your mother struck the match
Your father out for a walk down the lane.

The doors had all been shut
A cloth stuffed in my mouth
I writhed and I pleaded
But you were oblivious to my hurt.

I was burning, I was aflame!
Oh, the agony of it all
Then I fell unconscious
Feeling the searing, scorching pain.

The hospital walls, stark and white
My anxious parents faces
A constable sitting in one corner
I woke up to these sights.

You were there and your mother too
Pretending to be so kind
Your eyes warning me to be quiet
Threatening, sending a chill right through.

Your mother shoved the papers
In front of my face
"Sign these," she said
I asked what they contained.

"About your accident," she replied
"The stove burst
We had gone out
Your sasra found you," she lied.

So in fear I signed the dotted line
I hated myself for it
Why was I such a coward?
I cringed and wept inside.

Now I live in perpetual and constant fear
Back here in the house with you
Seeing the coldness in your eyes
Wondering whether my end is near.

My beautiful face is ugly and scarred
I cannot bear to see a mirror
My parents are shocked and hurt
My life has been marred.

I have been contemplating suicide
But I cannot hurt my parents so
They had raised me well
So my feelings will always be bottled inside.

'Sasra' is the Indian word for father-in-law.

On Physical Abuse

O woman, why do you cry alone in the dark
Weeping tears of frustration and shame?
Did he hurt you, abuse you, batter you up?
Did you let him do it again?

Rise up, shake off your shackles and be brave,
Bearer of life, you were born for great things.
Do you not know that you shape this society?
You were not born to bear only pain.

Teach your sons and your daughters both alike
Not to hurt or be hurt because of gender.
He was born male while you were born female,
In the scheme of things, does it really matter?

It isn't his fault, society's to blame
For teaching that woman's inferior.
Be loving yet firm, don't brook this nonsense
He will soon see reason again.

The world will be better when you work together
Man and woman, side by side.
Let's undo the wrongs of the past generations
Let us restore the girl child's pride.

Niloufer
2003

On Gossip

Women are fond of gossip
I've often heard it said.
Why this gender bias?
Why place it on women's head?

A group of college boys
Laughing inside the coffee shop
Have you heard their idle pratter?
Is that gossip, or not?

Some men at a stag party
What do they joke about?
Do they not also gossip?
What comes out of their mouths?

Sure, women do gossip too
But not all of the time
They share their experiences
And gossip, like men, when there is time.

આન્જી

On Ridicule

He called me dumb
"You are a woman", he said
"What would you know of such things?
Keep your tongue in check."

"Speak when you are spoken to
Do not presume to be
Highly intelligent and sensible
Your opinion means nothing to me."

"What do you know of business?
What do you know of finance?
Do you know the meaning of politics?
Go and wash your husband's pants."

"That's what woman was created for
To mend and cook and wash
Keep your foolish thoughts in your foolish head
All you can speak is hogwash."

Anger boiled inside me
Why should I listen to this?
I will go out into the world and show him
What a woman like me can achieve.

And so you see me now
In every walk of life, in every occupation
Look this way and that, look here and there
I, a woman, contributes equally to this nation.

From Girl Child To Woman

Waiting outside they heard the cries
What joy and anticipation in their eyes
A child has been born
A child has been born
It must be a boy, they all surmise.

Imagine the disappointment and sorrow
They will carry through all their tomorrows
A girl child's been born
A girl child's been born
Closing her eyes, the mother wept for her newborn.

Money does not grow on trees
It goes towards payment of her son's fees
This girl must stay home
This girl must stay home
And work in the house and toil with the grease.

"Mother, I want to go to school too", she pleads
"Hush, child, be grateful and don't show such greed."
You were born a girl
You were born a girl
The mother distressed, her poor heart bleeds.

Now grown up into a pretty, young maiden
With womanly skills, tresses with flowers laden
Now look for a boy
Now look for a boy
But what about dowry? O, what a burden!

Dressed up and parading her womanly skills
Of making chapattis, good food and pickles
Oh, what humiliation
Oh, what humiliation
Ask for her hand, which of these suitors will?

Waiting for approval and appreciation
Her parents can't hide their anticipation
Will there be dowry?
Will there be dowry?
The price is arranged after prolonged negotiation.

The ceremony is over, the bride has gone home
So much expense, her parents dry to the bone
Such is their fate
Such is their fate
Having a daughter, all their wealth gone.

Married now and leading a quiet life
Fairly comfortable, not much strife
But oh, so alone
But oh, so alone
He's with his work while she's a housewife.

After all she is but a woman and so
Can she think for herself? What does she know?
Leave her alone
Leave her alone
How far can the intelligence of a woman go?

And now that she has given birth to a boy
There's so much of rejoicing and so much of joy
A girl wasn't wanted
A girl wasn't wanted
The fools! Without a woman there would be no life.

One child after another, three males and a female
Wearied and haggard, her health down the drain
Suffer in silence
Suffer in silence
Oh woman, Oh woman, who feels your pain?

Awaken! Why do you allow yourself to suffer?
Awaken! By example, make your little girl tougher
Show her the way
Show her the way
Common sense should tell you there must be another.

Fight to educate her, give her the same food
Your sons and your daughter, they are all good
Give her equality
Give her equality
She will stand tall and straight, making you proud.

The Labour Class In Rajasthan

It's as if a festival of colour is on
The multi-coloured saris
The air filled with song
The bracelets and noserings
And multi-coloured things
As the women labour
Regardless of the sun.

The men, equally unique in dress
Languish sleepily
Under the trees
Digging their teeth
Taking shade from the sun
While their women labour on
They consider it their birthright, no less!

On Rape

Is there a man in this world
Who after committing this heinous deed
Could feel good about himself?

Forcing himself upon another
Loveless, senseless act of lust
Humiliating someone, using muscle power.

Does he really feel powerful?
Does he really feel strong?
Disgusting and filthy act of shame!

And when this ugly act is done
Does he stop to think of the repercussions
Not only on himself, if she complains?

What about that woman?
She was someone's daughter, someone's wife
Someone's mother. What will happen to her life?

She will carry with her always
Deep wounds and scars for life
She is repulsed; the horror lingers in her mind.

Who will help her find justice?
The legal system? Society? Who else?
They act as if she invited it.

Women's organisations
Sometimes help and take up the cause
And such men are put behind bars.

But the system made by and of men
Favours the rogue, the scoundrel
And makes little of such abused women.

You women, lift up your voices
Make yourselves heard; scream, shout if you have to
Be not afraid to bring such men to book.

They are the scum of society
Not fit to live amongst you and me
If I had my way, they'd hang from the nearest tree.

Learn self-defence, judo, karate
Be strong, be bold and brave
Lift your voices and mend this ailing society.

✥

The Girl Child

Her big brown eyes stared at him
As he sat wolfing down his food
Deep wells of emotion
Love, hurt, longing, pain
All reflected with such passion.

"Why don't you love me, papa?
Is it because I was born a girl?
Why do you love bhaiya?
You have all the time in the world
For him. For me, not an iota."

"Ma, I know you love me true
You feel for me, you understand
What I'm going through
Is it because as a girl
You had to carry this cross too?"

"It is almost as if you are afraid
To express your love for me
In front of Papa. I brought him shame
I was born a girl
Am I to blame?"

Her eyes filled with tears, pleading
Watching every move of her father
Her broken heart torn and bleeding
"Give me a chance, Papa
A girl I may be, but I am not a weakling."

"If I had your love
If you showed me kindness
It would motivate and spur me on
To great heights
I know deep down, I have the potential.

It is love I hunger for
It is anger that I feel
Frustration, depression trouble me
If you love me
I will grow!"

"Bhaiya" is the Indian word for brother.

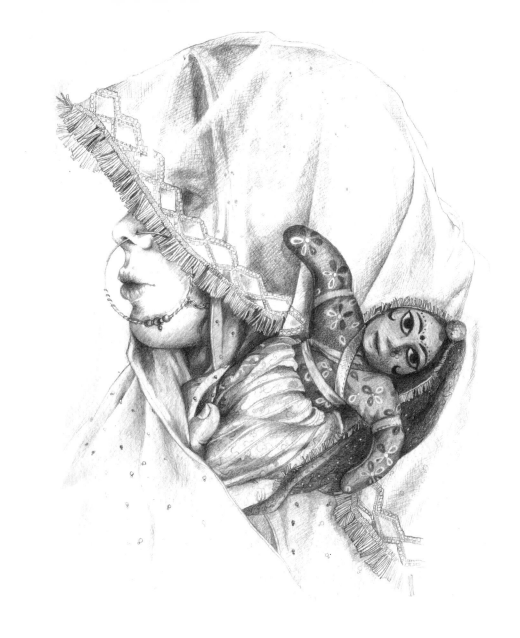

Child Bride

This old man was influential
One of the elders in the village
He was rich, and in a way special
Wise yet kind, that was his image.

My parents were having hard times
To make ends meet was tough
My father had taken to drinking
As if things were not hard enough!

I was only a little girl of eleven
When, one day, this old man came
It was late in the evening, past seven
He offered money to take me away.

Angry, afraid, hurt and unhappy
I watched, wide eyed, my parents accept
I was sold to this old man, his wife to be
I lay awake crying, while the world slept.

Hating him, I entered his home
A child bride for an old, old man
But day after day, he left me alone
He treated me well as anyone can.

He was kind, gentle, like a father to me
He bought me clothes and ornaments
He read to me, and taught me to read
And put me in school; he was God sent.

I took a long time to trust him
But as I grew, I knew
He had saved me from ruin
He had been wise and true.

A woman full grown, my gratitude
Was replaced with love and passion
I loved this old man with such magnitude
At last, I willingly made him my husband.

On Prostitution

Brazen hussy, standing there
Alone in the market place
Selling your wares.

Your look is cold and hard
You couldn't care less
And so you stand.

But as I look into your eyes
I feel your deep pain
Your outward stance is lies.

You try to cover your shame
But O, what can you do?
They say you are to blame.

What abject poverty?
What great distress?
What stark misery?

What drives you to this?

᨞᨞

For Granted

Of all God's creatures
A woman is
Taken for granted.

It's so easy to know
The seeds of
Her love forever planted.

From morn to night
She toils away
No one really notices.

All those things that
Just get done
Are taken for granted.

What stress has she?
Who understands?
Her task is never ending.

She asks for no thanks
Just your love
Her love is all encompassing.

Show her appreciation
Show your love
Don't take her for granted.

Dichotomy

At times, worshipped as Goddess
Revered and respected
At others, even branded a Witch
Evil seductress.

Talked and talked about
Pampered and loved
Hated and spurned
But never ignored.

At times, evoking passion
Sometimes, deep derision
Such conflicting emotions
Surround you, O Woman!

And yet you can never be
Ignored or forgotten
You are and always will be
In the pivotal position.

෨෮

International Women's Day

March 8
International Women's Day
Why?
Because I hold up half the sky!

I create life
I care and nurture, I love and I give
Why?
Because that is the very purpose of 'I'!

Like man
I contribute equally to the nation
Why?
Because efficient and capable am I!

I fought hard
To make my voice heard above the din
Why?
You weren't listening; it made me cry!

March 8
International Women's Day
Will be
To celebrate my creation, to make the world see!

Gently reminding
How uphill it has been
Everywhere
I am clearly visible, on land and in air!

March 8
International Women's Day -
Now, you know why
To remind you that I too hold up the sky!

Gender

Can two women see eye to eye?
Do they ever agree?
Legend has it that they are at loggerheads
Two women can never be

Friends, devoted, loyal and true.
I beg to differ!
Women are sensitive and caring
'Cause they also suffer

Like other women.
Women rule with their hearts
Men rule with their heads
Of one whole they are two parts.

Then why do we keep hearing
A woman this and a woman that?
The differences are needed
Haven't you heard, 'opposites attract'?

❧❧

ABOUT **THE DINSHAW J. AMARIA MEMORIAL FOUNDATION**

(Regd. No. F-15089 (Bombay). (Income Tax Exemption U/S 80G I.T. Act, 1961)

This registered, secular, Charitable Trust began in 1990 in the memory of the late Mr. Dinshaw Jamshedji Amaria (1910-1970), a self-made man who rose to a senior position by dint of sheer hard work. An orphan from the tender age of two, he had a heart of gold and could not bear to see suffering of any kind. Quietly, in his own small way, and silently but strongly supported by a loving wife, Dhun Dinshaw Amaria (1921-1992), he did what he could to help others.

The Dinshaw J. Amaria Memorial Foundation has served several needy persons with educational and medical assistance and has played a major role in rebuilding the Sri Budhanath High School at Balipatna and Girls High School at Banamalipur, Orrisa, damaged by the super cyclone in 1999. The schools have also been equipped with computers.

A father of four daughters, Mr. Dinshaw Amaria always maintained that there was no difference between boys and girls and that his daughters were equal to any boys anywhere. Therefore, it was appropriate that the Foundation in his memory took up the work of reconstructing the school for needy girls.

ABOUT **PASSAGES Association for Guidance, Education & Support** (Income Tax Exemption U/S 80G I.T. Act, 1961)

Established in 1998, PASSAGES is a non-profit, non-government organization working towards creating awareness in women about health and nutrition, and social and legal issues. A team of committed, dedicated and dynamic women from diverse fields of activity makes up the core committee of this organization.

It holds meaningful programmes for its members and for the public, has educational and awareness programmes for teenagers and adolescents, brings out an interesting quarterly Newsletter, undertakes research and has an ongoing Cancer project.

PASSAGES' cancer related activities include a dedicated Telephone Help Line for Breast Cancer (Tel. No. 98202 00300), a Medicine Bank, research, publications in English ('Whispering Hope'), Hindi ('Asha Ki Nayi Kiran') and Marathi ('Ashicha Ek Mridusanket'), a Support Group for Cancer and Counselling at Bombay Hospital, and Breast Cancer Awareness Camps all over the city.